Classical Japanese

Classical Japanese:
A Grammar

Exercise Answers and Tables

Haruo Shirane

Columbia University Press
New York

Columbia University Press
Publishers Since 1893
New York   Chichester, West Sussex

ISBN: 0-231-13530-0

∞

Columbia University Press books are printed on permanent and durable acid-free paper.
Printed in the United States of America
p 10 9 8 7 6 5 4 3 2 1

Contents

Classical Japanese

Grammar Exercise Answers

Chapter 2. Orthography and Pronunciation

Supply the modern Japanese orthography for the following words:

		Historical *kana*	English translation	Modern *kana*
Example	声	こゑ	Voice	こえ
1	藤原	ふぢはら	Clan name	ふじわら
2	水	みづ	Water	みず
3	思ふ	おもふ	To think	おもう
4	思ひ	おもひ	Thought, longing	おもい
5	思へ	おもへ	Think!	おもえ
6	男	をとこ	Man	おとこ
7	庵	いほり	Hut	いおり
8	今日	けふ	Today	きょう
9	京	きやう	Capital	きょう
10	少将	せうしやう	Lesser captain	しょうしょう
11	方位	はうゐ	Direction	ほうい
12	法会	ほふゑ	Memorial service	ほうえ
13	直衣	なほし	Robe	なおし

Chapter 3. Verbs

3.2 Regular Verbs

Conjugate the following *yodan* verbs:

	書_かく	知_しる	待_まつ	思_{おも}ふ
mizenkei	かか	しら	また	おもは
ren'yōkei	かき	しり	まち	おもひ
shūshikei	かく	しる	まつ	おもふ
rentaikei	かく	しる	まつ	おもふ
izenkei	かけ	しれ	まて	おもへ
meireikei	かけ	しれ	まて	おもへ

Conjugate the following *kami-ichidan* verbs:

	見_みる	似_にる	着_きる	顧_{かへり}みる
mizenkei	み	に	き	かへりみ
ren'yōkei	み	に	き	かへりみ
shūshikei	みる	にる	きる	かへりみる
rentaikei	みる	にる	きる	かへりみる
izenkei	みれ	にれ	きれ	かへりみれ
meireikei	みよ	によ	きよ	かへりみよ

Conjugate the following *shimo-ichidan* verb:

	蹴_ける
mizenkei	け
ren'yōkei	け
shūshikei	ける
rentaikei	ける
izenkei	けれ
meireikei	けよ

Conjugate the following *kami-nidan* verbs:

	落つ	尽く	恋ふ	忍ぶ
mizenkei	おち	つき	こひ	しのび
ren'yōkei	おち	つき	こひ	しのび
shūshikei	おつ	つく	こふ	しのぶ
rentaikei	おつる	つくる	こふる	しのぶる
izenkei	おつれ	つくれ	こふれ	しのぶれ
meireikei	おちよ	つきよ	こひよ	しのびよ

Conjugate the following *shimo-nidan* verbs:

	受く	捨つ	助く	眺む
mizenkei	うけ	すて	たすけ	ながめ
ren'yōkei	うけ	すて	たすけ	ながめ
shūshikei	うく	すつ	たすく	ながむ
rentaikei	うくる	すつる	たすくる	ながむる
izenkei	うくれ	すつれ	たすくれ	ながむれ
meireikei	うけよ	すてよ	たすけよ	ながめよ

Chapter 4. Irregular Verbs

4.1 Irregular Verbs

Conjugate the following *nahen* verbs:

	死ぬ	往ぬ (to leave)
mizenkei	しな	いな
ren'yōkei	しに	いに
shūshikei	しぬ	いぬ
rentaikei	しぬる	いぬる
izenkei	しぬれ	いぬれ
meireikei	しね	いね

Conjugate the following *rahen* verbs:

	有り	居り	侍り
mizenkei	あら	をら	はべら
ren'yōkei	あり	をり	はべり
shūshikei	あり	をり	はべり
rentaikei	ある	をる	はべる
izenkei	あれ	をれ	はべれ
meireikei	あれ	をれ	はべれ

Conjugate the following *kahen* verb:

	来
mizenkei	こ
ren'yōkei	き
shūshikei	く
rentaikei	くる
izenkei	くれ
meireikei	こ(よ)

Conjugate the following *sahen* verbs:

	す	ご覧ず	愛す
mizenkei	せ	ごらんぜ	あいせ
ren'yōkei	し	ごらんじ	あいし
shūshikei	す	ごらんず	あいす
rentaikei	する	ごらんずる	あいする
izenkei	すれ	ごらんずれ	あいすれ
meireikei	せよ	ごらんぜよ	あいせよ

Give the inflected form and the conjugation type of the underlined verbs.

1. 思ひ (*ren'yōkei* of *yodan* verb *omou*); 行か (*mizenkei* of *yodan* verb *yuku*).

2. のむ (*rentaikei* of *yodan* verb *nomu*).

3. 乗れ (*meireikei* of *yodan* verb *noru*).

4. 至り (*ren'yōkei* of *yodan* verb *itaru*).

5. いだす (*shūshikei* of *yodan* verb *idasu*).

6. 見ゆ (*shūshikei* of *shimo-nidan* verb *miyu*).

7. ゐ (*ren'yōkei* of *kami-ichidan* verb [w]*iru*).

8. 落つる (*rentaikei* of *kami-nidan* verb *otsu*); 落ち (*ren'yōkei* of *kami-nidan* verb *otsu*).

9. 死な (*mizenkei* of *nahen* verb *shinu*); 死ね (*meireikei* of *nahen* verb *shinu*).

Chapter 5. Adjectives and Adjectival Verbs

5.1 Adjectives

Conjugate the following *ku* adjectives:

Stem	多し ku	多し kari	無し ku	無し kari	赤し ku	赤し kari	高し ku	高し kari
MZ	○	おほから	○	なから	○	あかから	○	たかから
RY	おほく	おほかり	なく	なかり	あかく	あかかり	たかく	たかかり
SS	おほし	おほかり	なし	なかり	あかし	○	たかし	○
RT	おほき	おほかる	なき	なかる	あかき	あかかる	たかき	たかかる
IZ	おほけれ	おほかれ	なけれ	なかれ	あかけれ	○	たかけれ	○
MK	○	おほかれ	○	なかれ	○	あかかれ	○	たかかれ

Conjugate the following *shiku* adjectives:

Stem	嬉し (うれ) *shiku*	*shikari*	美し (うつく) *shiku*	*shikari*	をかし *shiku*	*shikari*	いみじ *shiku*	*shikari*
MZ	○	嬉しから	○	美しから	○	をかしから	○	いみじから
RY	嬉しく	嬉しかり	美しく	美しかり	をかしく	をかしかり	いみじく	いみじかり
SS	嬉し	○	美し	○	をかし	○	いみじ	○
RT	嬉しき	嬉しかる	美しき	美しかる	をかしき	をかしかる	いみじき	いみじかる
IZ	嬉しけれ	○	美しけれ	○	をかしけれ	○	いみじけれ	○
MK	○	嬉しかれ	○	美しかれ	○	をかしかれ	○	いみじかれ

5.2 Adjectival Verbs

Conjugate the following adjectival verbs:

	あからさまなり (brief, sudden)	あはれなり (moving)	はるかなり (distant)	おろかなり (stupid)
mizenkei	あからさまなら	あはれなら	はるかなら	おろかなら
ren'yōkei	あからさまなり あからさまに	あはれなり あはれに	はるかな はるかに	おろかな おろかに
shūshikei	あからさまなり	あはれなり	はるかなり	おろかなり
rentaikei	あからさまなる	あはれなる	はるかなる	おろかなる
izenkei	あからさまなれ	あはれなれ	はるかなれ	おろかなれ
meireikei	あからさまなれ	あはれなれ	はるかなれ	おろかなれ

	堂々たり （だうだう） (dignified)	茫々たり （ばうばう） (vast)	朧朧たり （ろうろう） (misty)
mizenkei	だうだうたら	ばうばうたら	ろうろうたら
ren'yōkei	だうだうたり だうだうと	ばうばうたり ばうばうと	ろうろうたり ろうろうと
shūshikei	だうだうたり	ばうばうたり	ろうろうたり
rentaikei	だうだうたる	ばうばうたる	ろうろうたる
izenkei	だうだうたれ	ばうばうたれ	ろうろうたれ
meireikei	だうだうたれ	ばうばうたれ	ろうろうたれ

Give the inflected form and the conjugation type of the underlined adjectives.

1. 近けれ（ちか） (*izenkei* of *ku* adjective); 乏しから（とも） (*mizenkei* of *shiku* adjective).

2. 煩はしかり（わづら） (*ren'yōkei* of *shiku* adjective); 事なく（こと） (*ren'yōkei* of *ku* adjective); 易かる（やす） (*rentaikei* of *ku* adjective); 心ぐるし（こころ） (*shūshikei* of *shiku* adjective).

3. わびしき (*rentaikei* of *shiku* adjective).

4. いみじう (*ren'yōkei* of *shiku* adjective *imiji*, "extreme"); いたう (*ren'yōkei* of *ku* adjective *itashi*, "intense").

Give the conjugation type and the inflected form of the underlined adjectival verbs.

1. はなやかに (*ren'yōkei* of *nari* adjectival verb); うれしげなる (*rentaikei* of *nari* adjectival verb); あはれなれ (*izenkei* of *nari* adjectival verb).

2. おろかなら (*mizenkei* of *nari* adjectival verb).

3. せちなる (*rentaikei* of *nari* adjectival verb).

4. 渺々と (*ren'yōkei* of *tari* adjectival verb); 曠 々 たり (*shūshikei* of *tari* adjectival verb).

5. あからさまに (*ren'yōkei* of *nari* adjectival verb).

6. 清らなる (*rentaikei* of *nari* adjectival verb).

7. 峨々と (*ren'yōkei* of *tari* adjectival verb); 索々たり (*shūshikei* of *tari* adjectival verb).

4.4 and 5.3.2A Sound changes in Verbs and Adjectives

Give the original form of the underlined sound-changed word.

1. 読うで, 泣いて.

2. 激しう, いみじう 赤う.

3. 等しかん なり.

4. よい 馬.

5. くんでうって.

Chapter 6. Negative and Recollective Auxiliary Verbs

6.1 Negative *ZU*

Conjugate the negative auxiliary verb *zu*.

mizenkei	○	○	ざら
ren'yōkei	○	ず	ざり
shūshikei	○	ず	○
rentaikei	ぬ	○	ざる
izenkei	ね	○	ざれ
meireikei	○	○	ざれ

Identify the inflected form of the underlined negative auxiliary verb *zu* in the following sentences:

1. *Ren'yōkei of zu.*

2. *Izenkei of zu.*

3. *Rentaikei of zu.*

Identify the inflected form of *zu* and translate the sentence into English.

1. *Shūshikei.* The flower does not bloom.

2. *Ren'yōkei.* People also did not appear.

3. *Shūshikei.* The boat cannot move forward.

4. *Shūshikei.* It makes absolutely no sound.

5. *Ren'yōkei.* S/he did not laugh at all.

6. *Rentaikei.* There is a bird that does not sing very much.

6.2.1 *KI*

Conjugate the recollective auxiliary verb *ki.*

mizenkei	◯
ren'yōkei	◯
shūshikei	き
rentaikei	し
izenkei	しか
meireikei	◯

Identify the conjugation and the inflection of the underlined verb and the inflection of the underlined *ki* auxiliary verb.

1. *Ki-shi* is the *ren'yōkei* of the *kahen* verb *ku,* "to go/come," and the *rentaikei* of the past-tense *ki,* modifying the noun *kata,* "direction." *Shi-ki* is the *ren'yōkei* of the *sahen* verb *su,* "to do," and the *shūshikei* of the past-tense *ki.*

2. *Furi* is the *ren'yōkei* of the *yodan* verb *furu,* "to fall." *Shika* is the *izenkei* of the recollective *ki. Ki* is the *shūshikei* of the recollective *ki.*

3. *Shi-ki* is the *ren'yōkei* of the *sahen* verb *su*, "to do," and the *shūshikei* of the past-tense *ki*.

4. *Kudari-shi* is the *ren'yōkei* of the *yodan* verb *kudaru*, "to leave (the capital)," and the *rentaikei* of the recollective *ki*, modifying the noun *toki*, "time." *Nakari-ki* is the *ren'yōkei* of the *ku* adjective *nashi*, "not have," and the *shūshikei* of the recollective *ki*.

6.2.2 *KERI*

Identify the function and its inflected form of the underlined section. If the underlined section is not the auxiliary verb *keri*, what is it?

1. *Ari-keri*: hearsay past in *shūshikei*; *nari-keru*: hearsay past in *rentaikei* (because of bound particle *namu*).

2. *Wasure-ni-keri*: direct past in *shūshikei*.

3. *Ki-ni-keri*: exclamatory recognition in *shūshikei*.

4. *Nari-ni-keri*: direct past in *shūshikei*.

5. *Kere*: *izenkei* ending of *shiku* adjective *namamekashi*, "romantic."

6. *Ari-kere-ba*: direct past in *izenkei* (following *ren'yōkei* of *rahen* verb *ari*, "to exist"; *ii-keri*: direct past in *shūshikei* (following *ren'yōkei* of *yodan* verb *iu*, "to say").

7. *Nari-keri*: exclamatory recognition in *shūshikei* (following *ren'yōkei* of copular *nari*).

Chapter 7. Perfective and Continuative Auxiliary Verbs

7.1 Auxiliary Verbs *NU* and *TSU*

Identify the function and the inflected form.

1. *Michi-nu*: perfective *nu* in *shūshikei*; *fuki-nu-beshi*: *nu* of certainty in *shūshikei*.

2. *Itari-nu*: perfective *nu* in *shūshikei*.

3. *Ire-tsu-beku*: confidence *tsu* in *shūshikei*.

4. *Nagashi-te-keri*: perfective *tsu* in *ren'yōkei* (following *ren'yōkei* of verb *nagasu*, "to throw in").

Fill in the conjugations for the perfective auxiliary verb *nu*.

mizenkei	な
ren'yōkei	に
shūshikei	ぬ
rentaikei	ぬる
izenkei	ぬれ
meireikei	ね

Identify the auxiliary verb or the verb and the inflected form of the underlined parts.

1. *Saki-nu*: certainty *nu* in *shūshikei*.

2. *Shira-nu*: negative auxiliary verb *zu* in *rentaikei* (modifying an implied *mono*).

3. *Fuke-nu*: perfective auxiliary verb *nu* in *shūshikei*; *kaeri-tamai-ne*: perfective auxiliary verb *nu* in *meireikei*.

4. *Ara-ne-domo*: negative auxiliary verb *zu* in *izenkei* (followed by conjunctive particle *domo*).

5. *Ine*: *nahen* verb *inu*, "to leave," in *meireikei*.

6. *Ki-nu*: perfective auxiliary verb *nu* in *shūshikei*; negative auxiliary verb *zu* in *rentaikei* (following *mizenkei* of *shimo-nidan* verb *tsukisu*, "to exhaust," and modifying *mono*, "thing").

7. *Mie-nu*: negative auxiliary verb *zu* in *rentaikei*; *omoi-tamai-ne*: perfective auxiliary verb *nu* in *meireikei*.

8. *Nara-ne-ba*: negative auxiliary verb *zu* in *izenkei*; *ara-zu*: *shūshikei* of negative *zu*.

9. *Omoi-yora-nu*: negative auxiliary verb *zu* in *rentaikei*; *kanai-nu*: perfective auxiliary verb *nu* in *shūshikei*.

10. *Ki-nu*: perfective auxiliary verb *nu* in *shūshikei*; *mie-ne-do*: negative auxiliary verb *zu* in *izenkei* (*mie-ne-domo* is *mizenkei* of *shimo-nidan* verb *miyu*, "to be visible," *izenkei* of *zu*, and conjunctive particle *domo*).

11. *Shira-nu*: negative auxiliary verb *zu* in *rentaikei*; *ara-ne-do*: negative auxiliary verb *zu* in *izenkei* (*ni wa ara-ne-do* is *ren'yōkei* of copular *nari*, bound particle *wa*, *izenkei* of *rahen* supplementary verb *ari*, *izenkei* of *zu*, and conjunctive particle *do*).

7.2.1 and 8.2 *TARI*

Identify the function and the inflected form.

1. *Kuwa-se-tare-domo*: perfective *tari* in *izenkei* (because of conjunctive particle *domo*).

2. *Hikari-tari*: continuative *tari* in *shūshikei*.

3. *Ke-nin tari-shi*: copular *tari* following a nominal and followed by *rentaikei* of recollective *ki*.

7.2.2 *RI*

Identify the function and the inflected form.

1. *Oe-ru*: continuative function, *rentaikei* of *ri* (following *izenkei* of verb *ou*, "to bear"); *yasume-ru*: continuative function, *rentaikei* of *ri* (following *izenkei* of verb *yasumu*, "to rest").

2. *Tate-ri-keru*: continuative/resultative function, *ren'yōkei* of *ri*; *yome-ru*: perfective function, *rentaikei* of *ri* (following *izenkei* of verb *yomu*, "to compose").

3. *Ie-re-ba*: perfective function, *izenkei* of *ri* (following *izenkei* of verb *iu*, "to say").

Chapter 9. Auxiliary Verbs of Speculation and Supposition

9.1 and 9.2 *MU* and *MUZU*

Identify the following functions:

1. Speculation.

2. Appropriateness, urging.

3. Intention.

4. Speculation/hypothetical/circumlocution; intentional.

5. Intentional; urging.

6. Speculation.

7. Circumlocution/hypothetical/speculation.

8. Speculation.

9.4 *RAMU*

Identify the function of the following examples of *ramu*:

1. Present speculation (*rentaikei* as a result of bound particle *ya*).

2. Causal speculation (*rentaikei*).

3. Present speculation (*rentaikei* as a result of bound particle *ya*).

4. Causal speculation (*izenkei* as a result of bound particle *koso*).

5. Hearsay (*rentaikei*, modifying the noun *yama*).

6. Circumlocution/present speculation (*rentaikei*, modifying the pronoun *koto*). (The speaker does not want to ask directly "what are you thinking?" and so asks in this roundabout, speculative way to be polite.)

9.5 *RASHI*

Underline the evidence for the supposition in the following sentences:

1. 春過ぎて夏来たるらし<u>白妙の 衣 干したり</u>天の香具山.

2. <u>立田川もみぢ葉流る</u>神なびの三室の山に時雨降るらし.

9.6 *MASHI*

Identify the function of *mashi* in the following examples:

1. Indecision.

2. Counterfactual speculation.

3. Counterfactual speculation.

4. Indecision.

5. Counterfactual speculation.

6. Desire for hypothetical state.

9.7 *BESHI*

Identify the function and the inflected form in the following examples:

1. Appropriateness/advice in *ren'yōkei*; appropriateness/advice in *ren'taikei*.

2. Potential in *mizenkei*.

3. Strong intention in *shūshikei*.

4. Conjecture with confidence in *shūshikei*.

5. Appropriateness/natural expectation in *rentaikei*.

6. Potential in *mizenkei*.

7. Potential, *mizenkei*.

8. Conjecture with confidence in *ren'yōkei*.

9. Strong intention in *shūshikei*.

10. Appropriateness/natural expectation/obligation in *rentaikei*.

9.8 *MERI*

Identify the function and the inflected form in the following sentences:

1. *A-mere*: visual supposition, *izenkei*.

2. *Iu-mere*: circumlocution, *izenkei*.

3. *Ōka-mere*: circumlocution, *izenkei*.

4. *Na-meri:* visual supposition, *shūshikei*.

5.2.1, 8.1, and 9.9 Different Examples of *NARI*

Identify the type or function of the *nari* and the inflected form in the following sentences:

1. *Nari* adjectival verb, *rentaikei*; copular *nari*, *shūshikei*.

2. Aural supposition/direct hearing *nari*, *shūshikei*; copular *nari*, *ren'yōkei*. (The first *nari* follows the *shūshikei* of the *kahen* verb *ku*, while the second copular *nari* follows the *rentaikei* of the *sahen* verb *owasu*, "to be, to arrive.")

3. Copular *nari*, *shūshikei*; copular *nari*, *ren'yōkei*.

4. Hearsay *nari*, *rentaikei*.

5. Aural supposition/direct hearing *nari*, *shūshikei*.

6. Direct hearing *nari*, *shūshikei*.

7. *Yodan* verb *naru*, "to become," *ren'yōkei*; hearsay *nari*, *shūshikei*.

8. *Nari* adjectival verb, *rentaikei*; copular *nari*, *shūshikei*.

Chapter 10. Negative Speculative, Desiderative, and Comparative Auxiliary Verbs

10.1.1 and 10.1.2 *JI* and *MAJI*

Identify the function and the inflected form of the underlined parts in the following sentences:

1. Negative intention, *shūshikei*.

2. Negative potential, *rentaikei*.

3. Inappropriateness, *rentaikei*.

4. Negative speculation, *shūshikei*.

5. Negative intention, *shūshikei*.

6. Negative intention, *shūshikei*.

7. Negative intention, *shūshikei*.

8. Inappropriateness/negative recommendation, *rentaikei*.

9. Negative command/prohibition, *rentaikei*.

10.2.1 and 10.2.2 *TASHI* and *MAHOSHI*

Identify the function and the inflected form in the following sentences:

1. *Takere*: first-person desire, *izenkei* (as a result of emphatic bound particle *koso*).

2. *Mise-mahoshi*: first-person desire, *shūshikei*.

3. *Ara-mahoshikaru-bekere*: situational wish, *rentaikei*. (This can also be considered the *rentaikei* of the *shiku* adjective *aramahoshi*, "ideal," since the *rahen* verb *ari*, "to be," does not refer to a living creature.)

Chapter 11. Passive-Causative Auxiliary Verbs

11.1 and 18.4.1 *RU* and *RARU*

Identify the function and the inflection of the underlined parts and the inflection of the verb that the auxiliary verb follows.

1. *Mi-ire-rare-zu*: potential, *mizenkei*, following *mizenkei*.

2. *Kaera-re-kere*: honorific, *ren'yōkei*, following *mizenkei*.

3. *Nora-ru-beki*: honorific, *shūshikei*, following *mizenkei*.

4. *Warawa-re-nu*: passive, *mizenkei*, following *mizenkei*.

5. *Omoi-ide-raru*: spontaneous, *shūshikei*, following *mizenkei*.

11.2 and 18.4.2 *SU, SASU, and SHIMU*

Identify the function and the inflection of the underlined parts in the following sentences:

1. *Ira-se-tamae*: honorific, *ren'yōkei* (followed by honorific supplementary verb *tamau*).

2. *Torae-sase-mu*: causative, *mizenkei*.

3. *Nukeide-sase-tamae-ri*: honorific, *ren'yōkei*. (*Nukeide-sase-tamae-ri* is the *ren'yōkei* of the *shimo-nidan* verb *nukeizu*, "to stand out," the *ren'yōkei* of the honorific auxiliary verb *sasu*, the *izenkei* of the honorific supplementary verb *tamau*, and the *shūshikei* of the auxiliary verb *ri*, creating a double honorific.)

4. *Se-shime-tamau*: honorific, *ren'yōkei* (followed by honorific supplementary verb *tamau*).

5. *Idasa-se-te*: causative, *ren'yōkei* (followed by conjunctive particle *te*); *utawa-se-tamau*: causative, *ren'yōkei* (followed by honorific supplementary verb *tamau*).

Chapter 12. Case Particles

12.6 *TO*

Identify the function of the underlined particles in the following sentences:

1. Result of change.

2. Action taken with another; citation.

3. Metaphor.

4. Parallel items.

5. Citation.

12.7 *YORI*

Identify the function of the underlined particle *yori* in the following sentences:

1. Point of origin/point of transit.

2. Means/method.

3. Rapid sequence.

4. Standard of comparison.

5. Restriction/limitation.

12.10 *NITE*

Identify the particular function of *nite* in the following sentences:

1. Indicates place.

2. Indicates age.

3. Indicates means.

4. Indicates cause.

Chapter 13. Conjunctive Particles

13.1 *BA*

Identify the function of the underlined *ba* in the following sentences and the inflected form that it follows:

1. General rule/temporal, *izenkei*.

2. General rule/temporal, *izenkei*; causal, *izenkei*.

3. Temporal, *izenkei*.

4. Hypothetical, *mizenkei*.

13.2 and 13.3 *TO, TOMO* and *DO, DOMO*

Identify the function of the underlined conjunctive particle and the inflected form that it follows.

1. Direct concessive, *izenkei*.

2. Hypothetical concessive, *shūshikei* of *rahen* verb *ari*.

3. Direct concessive, *izenkei*.

13.4, 13.5, and 13.6 *NI, O, GA,* and *TE*

Identify the functions of the underlined conjunctive particles in the following sentences:

1. Temporal/sequential connection, *rentaikei.*

2. Concessive connection, *rentaikei.*

3. Temporal/sequential connection, *ren'yōkei.*

12.1, 12.2, and 13.5 *GA* and *NO* as Case and Conjunctive Particles

Identify the functions of *ga* and *no* in the following sentences:

1. *Ga* as attributive marker; *no* as subject marker.

2. *No* as attributive marker; *no* as subject marker; *no* as implied nominal.

3. *No* as attributive marker; *ga* as concessive conjunctive particle.

4. *No* as subject marker; *ga* as implied nominal (following *rentaikei,* which is a nominalizer).

5. *No* as subject marker (followed by *rentaikei* of the verb *naru,* "to become").

12.3 and 13.4 *O* as a Case or Conjunctive Particle

Identify the type and function of the underlined particles in the following sentences:

1. Case particle, point of transit.

2. Case particle, object of action.

3. Conjunctive particle, cause.

12.9 and 13.6 Various Types of *SHITE*

Identify the type and function of *shite* in the following:

1. Case particle, acting together.

2. *Ren'yōkei* of *sahen* verb *su* and conjunctive particle *te.*

3. Conjunctive particle, parallel connection ("and").

4. Case particle, means/method.

13.8 *TSUTSU*

Identify the function of the underlined *tsutsu* in the following sentences:

1. Simultaneous action.

2. Continuous action.

13.9 *NAGARA*

Identify the function of *nagara* in the following sentences:

1. Simultaneous, parallel action.

2. Simultaneous, parallel action.

3. Concession.

12.4 and 13.4 *NI* as a Case and Conjunctive Particle

Identify the type and function of the particle *ni* in the following sentences:

1. Case particle, standard of comparison.

2. Case particle, cause of action; case particle, time of action; case particle, result of a change.

3. Conjunctive particle, concessive.

4.1.1, 5.2.1, 7.1.1, 8.1, 12.4, and 13.4 Six Possibilities for *NI*

Identify the type of *ni* in the following sentences:

1. Case particle *ni*, indicating cause of action; *ren'yōkei* of perfective auxiliary verb *nu*; conjunctive particle *ni*, indicating cause; and case particle *ni*, indicating result of change.

2. *Ren'yōkei* of adjectival verb *komayaka-nari*.

Chapter 14. Bound Particles

14.4, 14.5, 14.5A, 14.6, 14.6A, and 14.7 *ZO, NAMU (NAN), YA (YAWA), KA (KAWA),* and *KOSO*

Identify the bound particle (*kakari-joshi*), the inflected bound ending, and the function of the bound particle.

> 1. *Zo, rentaikei* of *sahen* verb *su,* emphatic.
>
> 2. *Namu, rentaikei* of *rahen* polite supplementary verb *haberi,* emphatic.
>
> 3. *Ya, rentaikei* of auxiliary verb *ramu,* doubt.
>
> 4. *Yawa, rentaikei* of auxiliary verb *beshi,* rhetorical question.
>
> 5. *Ka, rentaikei* of speculative auxiliary *mu,* question.
>
> 6. *Kawa, rentaikei* of speculative auxiliary verb *mu,* rhetorical question.
>
> 7. *Koso, izenkei* of negative auxiliary verb *zu,* emphatic.
>
> 8. *Zo, rentaikei* of negative auxiliary verb *zu,* emphatic.
>
> 9. *Zo, rentaikei* of *shiku* adjective (*imiji*), emphatic (followed by interjectory particle *ya*).
>
> 10. *Ka, rentaikei* of perfective auxiliary verb *nu,* question.
>
> 11. *Namu* (*nan*)*, rentaikei* of auxiliary verb *keri,* emphatic.
>
> 12. *Yawa, rentaikei* of *yodan* verb *omou,* "to think," rhetorical question.

14.2 *MO*

Identify the function carried out by the underlined particle *mo* in the following sentences:

> 1. Emphatic.
>
> 2. Incremental.
>
> 3. Parallel listing.

14.5, 14.5A, 14.6, and 14.6A *YA (YAWA)* and *KA (KAWA)*

Identify the function of *ya, yawa* and *ka, kawa* in the following sentences:

> 1. Doubt/interrogative.
>
> 2. Rhetorical question.
>
> 3. Rhetorical question.

14.7 *KOSO*

Identify the function of *koso* and the bound part in the following sentences:

      1. Concessive, *ne* (*izenkei* of negative auxiliary verb *zu*).

      2. Anxiety over outcome (in *mo koso* combination), *are* (*izenkei* of *rahen* verb *ari*, "to have").

      3. Strong emphatic, *kere* (*izenkei* of auxiliary verb *keri*). (*Ni* is *ren'yōkei* of copular *nari*).

Chapter 15. Adverbial Particles

15.2 *DANI*

Identify the function of *dani* in the following sentences:

      1. Minimal desire/need.

      2. Analogy (giving lesser example to emphasize something greater).

      3. Analogy (giving lesser example to emphasize something greater).

15.3 *SAE*

Identify the function of *sae* in the following sentences:

      1. Addition.

      2. Analogy (even the sight of crows is moving, *let alone more elegant birds*).

      3. Addition.

15.4 and 15.5 *NOMI* and *BAKARI*

Identify the functions of the underlined particles in the following sentences:

      1. *Bakari*: degree/extent.

      2. *Bakari*: estimation.

      3. *Nomi*: emphasis or restriction.

      4. *Nomi*: restriction.

15.6 *NADO*

Identify the function of *nado* in the following:

1. Circumlocution. Since rain is the only important subject here, "and such" is circumlocution.

2. Example from a longer list.

15.7 *MADE*

Identify the function of the underlined *made* in the following sentences:

1. (Spatial) end point.

2. (Temporal) end point.

3. Unexpected extent or degree.

15.8 *SHI, SHIMO*

Identify both the function of the underlined particle and the word or part of the sentence that is being emphasized.

1. Emphasis, with emphasis on previous word *ima* (now).

2. Emphatic negation, with emphasis on lack of a strong guardian.

3. Emphatic negation, with emphasis on death not coming from the front.

Chapter 16. Final and Interjectory Particles

16.1.4 *SO*

Identify the verb and the inflection that precedes *so* in the following sentences:

1. *Ren'yōkei* of *yodan* verb *ariku*, "to walk around."

2. *Mizenkei* of *sahen* verb *su*, "to do."

3. *Ren'yōkei* of honorific verb *notamau*, "to speak."

16.1.8, 16.1.9, and 16.1.10 (MO)GANA, TESHIGA(NA), and NISHIGA(NA)

Identify the function of the underlined final particle and the grammatical form that it follows.

1. Desire unlikely to be fulfilled, following the nominal *hito*, "person."

2. First-person desire, following *ren'yōkei* of *shimo-nidan* verb *u*, "to obtain."

3. First-person desire, following *ren'yōkei* of *rahen* verb *ari*, "to be."

4. Desire unlikely to be fulfilled, following the nominal *waza*, "way."

16.1.1 and 16.1.5 KANA and KASHI

Identify the function of the final particle and the grammatical form that it follows.

1. Exclamatory *kana*, following *rentaikei* of perfective auxiliary verb *tsu*.

2. Emphatic, following *shūshikei* of speculative auxiliary verb *mu*.

3. Exclamatory *kana*, following nominal noun *mono*.

16.1.2 and 16.1.3 Two Kinds of Final Particle NA

Identify the function of the underlined particle *na* and the inflected form that it follows.

1. Prohibition, following *shūshikei* of *kahen* verb *ku*, "to come."

2. Exclamation, following *shūshikei* of adjective *kanashi*, "sad."

3. Prohibition, *shūshikei* of *yodan* verb *morasu*, "to let out."

4. Seeking confirmation, *shūshikei* of speculative auxiliary verb *meri*.

14.4 and 16.1.6 Different Functions of NAMU

Identify the type of *namu* and the grammatical form that it follows.

1. *Mizenkei* of perfective auxiliary verb *nu* and of auxiliary verb *mu*, indicating strong intention.

2. *Mizenkei* of *nahen* verb *inu*, "to leave," and intentional auxiliary verb *mu*.

3. Desiderative final particle *namu*, following *mizenkei* of *yodan* verb *fuku*, "to blow."

4. Emphatic bound particle *namu*, bound at the end with *rentaikei* of auxiliary verb *keri*.

5. Desiderative final particle *namu*, following *mizenkei* of *yodan* verb *saku*, "to bloom."

16.1.7 BAYA

Identify the type of *baya* and the grammatical form that it follows.

1. Conjunctive bound particle *ba*, following *izenkei* of *sahen* verb *su*, "to do" (combined here with a nominal to form the verb *momiji-su*, "to turn bright colors"), and doubt bound paricle *ya*.

2. Desiderative final particle *baya*, following *mizenkei* of *yodan* verb *iku*, "to go."

3. Desiderative final particle *baya*, following *mizenkei* of humble *yodan* verb *uke-tamawaru*, "to hear."

Chapter 17. Nouns, Pronouns, Adverbs, Interjections, Conjunctions, and Attributive Words

17.1 and 17.2 Nouns and Pronouns

Identify the type of nominal: common noun, proper noun, numerical noun, nominal noun, or pronoun.

1. <u>その</u>　<u>日</u>，やうやく<u>草加</u>という <u>宿</u> にたどり着きにけり．
　　pronoun　common noun　　　　　　proper noun　　　　common noun

2. <u>ひとり</u>のみ ながむるよりはをみなへし <u>わ</u>が住む <u>宿</u> に植ゑて見ましを．
　numerical noun　　　　　　　　　　　　　　pronoun　　common noun

17.3 Adverbs

Identify the type of adverb and the word or phrase that is being modified by that adverb.

1. たれも<u>いまだ</u> 都 慣れぬほどにて <u>え</u> 見つけず．*Imada* is a negative adverb correlated with the negative auxiliary verb *zu* to mean "not yet." *E* is a negative adverb correlated with the negative auxiliary verb *zu*, to mean "cannot."
　　　correlated　　　　　　　　　correlated

2. <u>ほのぼのと</u> 春こそ空に <u>来</u>にけらし天の香具山かすみたなびく．*Honobono* is a circumstantial adverb, meaning "slightly" or "faintly," describing the condition created by the action of *kinikerashi*, "to appear to have come."
　circumstantial

3. 猛き 心 つかふ人も，<u>よも</u> <u>あらじ</u>．*Yomo* is a negative adverb, "absolutely," combined with the negative speculative auxiliary verb *ji* to mean "cannot exist at all."
　　　　　　　　　correlated

4. <u>やうやう</u>白く<u>なり行く</u>，山ぎはすこしあかりて．*Yōyō* is an adverb indicating
　degree

the degree of change expressed by *nariyuku*, "to turn." *Yōyō* could also be interpreted as a circumstantial adverb.

17.6 Attributive Words

Identify the following attributive words and give their meaning:

1. *Sashitaru*, "that much."

2. *Saru*, "like that."

3. *Aru*, "a certain."

4. *Kakaru*, "this kind of."

Chapters 18 and 19. Honorific, Humble, and Polite Expressions

18 and 19 Honorific Supplementary Verbs

Identify the type of the honorific supplementary verb and give the inflected form.

1. 奉り: *ren'yōkei* of humble *tatematsuru*; 給ひ: *ren'yōkei* of honorific *tamau*.

2. めす: *shūshikei* of honorific *mesu*.

3. 給へ: *meireikei* of honorific *tamau*.

4. きこえ: *ren'yōkei* of humble *kikoyu*.

18 and 19 Honorific Verbs

Select the honorific, humble, and polite verbs that best match the following modern honorific expressions.

1. おはす, おはします

2. 思す, おぼしめす

3. 仰す, 宣ふ

4. ご覧ず

5. 給ふ (yodan)

6. 聞こしめす

　　7. 知(し)ろしめす

　　8. 聞(き)こしめす, めす

　　9. 遊(あそ)ばす

　　10. 大殿(おほとの)ごもる

　　11. めす

18.3.1, 18.4.2, and 19.1.8 Supplementary *TAMAU* and Auxiliary Verb *SU*

In the following sentences, identify the function of the supplementary verb *tamau* and the auxiliary verb *su*, and identify the inflected forms:

1. 書(か)か ___せ___ 給(給) へ り .
   <small>honorific ren'yōkei honorific izenkei</small>

2. 助(たす)け た ま へ .
   <small>honorific meireikei</small>

3. 入(い)ら ___せ___ 給(給) へ .
   <small>honorific ren'yōkei honorific meireikei</small>

4. よま ___せ___ 給(給) ふ .
   <small>causative ren'yōkei honorific shūshikei</small>

5. 聞(き)き 給(給) へ て .
   <small>humble ren'yōkei</small>

18.2 and 18.3 Honorific Supplementary Verbs Versus Honorific Verbs

Indicate whether the underlined word is an honorific verb or an honorific supplementary verb, and give its inflection. If it is an honorific verb, what is its meaning?

1. *Ren'yōkei* of honorific verb *tamau*, "to give/bestow"; *mizenkei* of honorific verb *tamau*, "to give/bestow."

2. *Mizenkei* of honorific supplementary verb *tamau*; *shūshikei* of honorific supplementary verb *tamau*.

3. *Shūshikei* of honorific verb *owasu*, "to be."

4. *Shūshikei* of honorific supplementary verb *owasu*.

5. *Ren'yōkei* of honorific verb *owasu*, "to be" (followed by *izenkei* of past *keri*).

Chapter 19. Humble and Polite Expressions

19.1 and 19.4 Humble and Polite Verbs

Select the honorific, humble, and polite verbs that best match the following modern humble expressions.

1. 申^{まう}す, 聞^きこゆ

2. 奉^{たてまつ}る, 参^{まゐ}らす

3. 賜^{たまは}る, 給^{たま}ふ (*shimo-nidan*), 承^{うけたまは}る

4. 参^{まゐ}る

5. 罷^{まか}る, まかづ

6. はべり, さぶらふ, さふらふ, 仕^{つかまつ}る

7. 致^{いた}す, 仕^{つかまつ}る

8. 承^{うけたまは}る

18.3, 19.1, and 19.4 Distinguishing Among Honorific, Humble, and Polite Verbs

Identify the type of honorific verb and give the *shūshikei* form and the meaning.

1. Humble, まうす, to say; honorific, おはします, to be.

2. Polite, はべり, to be; humble, きこゆ, to say.

3. Honorific, きこしめす, to hear; honorific, のたまふ, to say.

4. Humble, うけたまはる, to hear; polite, はべり, to be.

5. Honorific, おぼす, to think/feel.

6. Humble, たてまつる, to give.

19.1 Humble Verbs Versus Humble Supplementary Verbs

Determine whether the underlined units in the following sentences are humble verbs or humble supplementary verbs, and identify their inflection. If it is a humble verb, what is its meaning?

1. *Ren'yōkei* of humble verb *makazu,* "to take one's leave" (from a place of high status).

2. *Rentaikei* of *yodan* humble verb *mōsu,* "to say." (*Ni* is a conjunctive particle.)

3. *Mizenkei* of humble supplementary verb *mōsu.*

4. *Izenkei* of *yodan* humble verb *saburō,* "to serve a person of high status."

5. *Ren'yōkei* of humble verb *uketamawaru,* "to hear," "to receive from a person of higher status."

Appendix 5. Rhetorical Techniques in Japanese Poetry

Identify the *makura-kotoba* or *jokotoba* in the following two poems. If it is a *makura-kotoba,* what does it modify? If it is a *jokotoba,* how is it linked to the main body?

1. The *makura-kotoba* is *chihayaburu,* which modifies *kamiyo* (age of the gods).

2. The *jokotoba* is *Suruga naru Utsu no yamabe no,* which is linked to the main body by the word *utsutsu* (reality), which phonically echoes the place-name Utsu.

Identify the *engo* and *kakekotoba* in the following poem:

1. The *kakekotoba* are *nagisa* (shore) and *naki* (not . . . to meet); and *urami* (gazing at a bay), *urami* (resentment), and *miru* (to see). The *engo* are *nami* (wave) and *yoru* (to approach), *tachikaeru* (to return), *urami* (bay), and *nagisa* (shore)—all of which are related to water.

Appendix 7. Auxiliary Verb Combinations

Identify the following auxiliary verb compounds, their functions, and their inflected forms:

1. *Tsu-beki:* *shūshikei* of certainty *tsu* and *rentaikei* of speculative *beshi* (conjecture with confidence), indicating strong expectation.

2. *Tsu-beku*: *shūshikei* of certainty *tsu* and *ren'yōkei* of potential *beshi*, indicating certainty about potential.

3. *Nu-beshi*: *shūshikei* of certainty *nu* and *shūshikei* of speculative *beshi* (conjecture with confidence), indicating strong certainty about future; *te-n*: *mizenkei* of certainty *tsu* and *shūshikei* of intentional *mu* (with sound change to *n*), indicating strong intention.

4. *Na-n*: *mizenkei* of certainty *nu* and *shūshikei* of speculative *mu* (with sound change to *n*), indicating strong certainty about future.

5. *Te-keri*: *ren'yōkei* of perfective *tsu* and *shūshikei* of recollective *keri*, indicating exclamatory recognition of completed action.

6. *Te-shi*: *ren'yōkei* of perfective *tsu* and *rentaikei* of recollective *ki*, indicating completed action; *te-ki*: *ren'yōkei* of perfective *tsu* and *shūshikei* of recollective *ki*, indicating completed action.

7. *Tari-keru*: *ren'yōkei* of resultative *tari* and *rentaikei* of recollective *keri*, indicating resultative past.

Tables of Grammatical Forms

Table I

VERB CONJUGATIONS

Conjugation	Row	Verb	Stem	MZ	RY	SS	RT	IZ	MR
yodan	カ	書く	か	-か	-き	-く	-く	-け	-け
	ガ	泳ぐ	およ	-が	-ぎ	-ぐ	-ぐ	-げ	-げ
	サ	移す	うつ	-さ	-し	-す	-す	-せ	-せ
	タ	打つ	う	-た	-ち	-つ	-つ	-て	-て
	ハ	思ふ	おも	-は	-ひ	-ふ	-ふ	-へ	-へ
	バ	呼ぶ	よ	-ば	-び	-ぶ	-ぶ	-べ	-べ
	マ	読む	よ	-ま	-み	-む	-む	-め	-め
	ラ	取る	と	-ら	-り	-る	-る	-れ	-れ
shimo-ichidan	カ	蹴る	(け)	け	け	ける	ける	けれ	けよ
shimo-nidan	ア	得	(う)	え	え	う	うる	うれ	えよ
	カ	受く	う	-け	-け	-く	-くる	-くれ	-けよ
	ガ	告ぐ	つ	-げ	-げ	-ぐ	-ぐる	-ぐれ	-げよ
	サ	寄す	よ	-せ	-せ	-す	-する	-すれ	-せよ
	ザ	混ず	ま	-ぜ	-ぜ	-ず	-ずる	-ずれ	-ぜよ
	タ	捨つ	す	-て	-て	-つ	-つる	-つれ	-てよ
	ダ	出づ	い	-で	-で	-づ	-づる	-づれ	-でよ
	ナ	尋ぬ	たづ	-ね	-ね	-ぬ	-ぬる	-ぬれ	-ねよ
	ハ	教ふ	をし	-へ	-へ	-ふ	-ふる	-ふれ	-へよ
	バ	述ぶ	の	-べ	-べ	-ぶ	-ぶる	-ぶれ	-べよ
	マ	求む	もと	-め	-め	-む	-むる	-むれ	-めよ
	ヤ	消ゆ	き	-え	-え	-ゆ	-ゆる	-ゆれ	-えよ
	ラ	流る	なが	-れ	-れ	-る	-るる	-るれ	-れよ
	ワ	植う	う	ゑ	ゑ	う	うる	うれ	ゑよ
kami-ichidan	カ	着る	(き)	き	き	きる	きる	きれ	きよ
	ナ	似る	(に)	に	に	にる	にる	にれ	によ
	ハ	干る	(ひ)	ひ	ひ	ひる	ひる	ひれ	ひよ
	マ	見る	(み)	み	み	みる	みる	みれ	みよ
	ヤ	射る	(い)	い	い	いる	いる	いれ	いよ
	ワ	居る	(ゐ)	ゐ	ゐ	ゐる	ゐる	ゐれ	ゐよ

Conjugation	Row	Verb	Stem	MZ	RY	SS	RT	IZ	MR
kami-nidan	カ	起く	おす	-き	-き	-く	-くる	-くれ	-きよ
	ガ	過ぐ	く	-ぎ	-ぎ	-ぐ	-ぐる	-ぐれ	-ぎよ
	タ	朽つ	は	-ち	-ち	-つ	-つる	-つれ	-ちよ
	ダ	恥づ		-ぢ	-ぢ	-づ	-づる	-づれ	-ぢよ
	ハ	強ふ	し	-ひ	-ひ	-ふ	-ふる	-ふれ	-ひよ
	バ	伸ぶ	の	-び	-び	-ぶ	-ぶる	-ぶれ	-びよ
	マ	恨む	うら	-み	-み	-む	-むる	-むれ	-みよ
	ヤ	悔ゆ	く	-い	-い	-ゆ	-ゆる	-ゆれ	-いよ
	ラ	下る	お	-り	-り	-る	-るる	-るれ	-りよ
rahen	ラ	有り	あ	-ら	-り	-り	-る	-れ	-れ
nahen	ナ	死ぬ	し	-な	-に	-ぬ	-ぬる	-ぬれ	-ね
kahen	カ	来	(く)	こ	き	く	くる	くれ	こよ
sahen	サ	す	(す)	せ	し	す	する	すれ	せよ

Table 2

ADJECTIVES AND ADJECTIVAL VERB FORMS

Conjuga-tions	Example	Stem	MZ	RY	SS	RT	IZ	MR
ku adj.	清し	きよ	○	-く	-し	-き	-けれ	○
			-から	-かり	○	-かる	○	-かれ
shiku adj.	美し	うつく	○	-しく	-し	-しき	-しけれ	○
			-しから	-しかり	○	-しかる	○	-しかれ
	いみじ	いみ	○	-じく	-じ	-じき	-じけれ	○
			-じから	-じかり	○	-じかる	○	-じかれ
nari adj. verb	静かなり	しづか	-なら	-なり	-なり	-なる	-なれ	-なれ
			○	-に	○	○	○	○
tari adj. verb	堂々たり	だうだう	-たら	-たり	-たり	-たる	-たれ	-たれ
			○	-と	○	○	○	○

Table 3

SOUND CHANGES

Verbs

i-sound change	u-sound change	Nasalized sound change	Compressed sound change
Ki, gi, and *shi* in *yodan* become *i*	*Hi, bi,* and *mi* in *yodan* become *u*	*Bi* and *mi* in *yodan* and *ni* in *nihan* become *n* followed by voiced particle (*de*) or auxiliary verb (*dari*)	*Chi, hi,* and *ri* in *yodan* and *ri* in *rahen* become *tsu*

急_{いそ}ぎて
↓
急いで

歌_{うた}ひて
↓
歌うて

学_{まな}びて
↓
学んで

失_{うしな}ひて
↓
失つて
↓
失つて

Adjectives

i-sound change	u-sound change	Nasalized sound change
Ki in *ku* and *shiku* adjectives becomes *i*	*Ku* in *ku* and *shiku* adjectives becomes *u*	Final *ru* of adjectives in *rentaikei* and adjectival verbs becomes *n* when followed by auxiliary verb like *meri* or *nari*

白_{しろ}き雲_{くも}
↓
白い雲

若_{わか}く
↓
若う

多かるめり
↓
多かんめり

Table 4

AUXILIARY VERB CONJUGATIONS

Aux. verb	Functions	MZ	RY	SS	RT	IZ	MR	Conj.	Follows
る (11.1)	Spontaneous, potential, passive, honorific	れ	れ	る	るる	るれ	れよ	*shimo-nidan*	MZ of YD, NH, RH verbs
らる (11.1)		られ	られ	らる	らるる	らるれ	られよ		MZ of verbs other than the above
す (11.2)		せ	せ	す	する	すれ	せよ		MZ of YD, NH, RH verbs
さす (11.2)	Causative, honorific	させ	させ	さす	さする	さすれ	させよ		MZ of verbs other than the above
しむ (11.2)		しめ	しめ	しむ	しむる	しむれ	しめよ		MZ
つ (7.1.2)	Perfective, certainty, parallel	て	て	つ	つる	つれ	てよ	*shimo-nidan*	
ぬ (7.1.1)		な	に	ぬ	ぬる	ぬれ	ね	*nahen*	RY
たり (7.2.1)	Resultative, continuative, perfective, parallel	たら	たり	たり	たる	たれ	たれ	*rahen*	
り (7.2.2)	Resultative, certainty, perfective	ら	り	り	る	れ	れ		IZ of YD, MZ of SH
き (6.2.1)	Personal past	(せ)	○	き	し	しか	○	Special	RY (special after KH and SH)
けり (6.2.2)	Hearsay past, exclamatory recognition, direct past	(けら)	○	けり	ける	けれ	○	*rahen*	RY
む (9.1)	Speculation, intention, appropriateness, urging, circumlocution, hypothetical	(ま) / ○	○ / ○	む / (ん)	む / (ん)	め / ○	○ / ○	*yodan*	MZ
むず (9.2)	Intention, speculation	○ / ○	○ / ○	むず / (んず)	むずる / (んずる)	むずれ / (んずれ)	○ / ○	*sahen*	
らむ (9.4)	Present speculation, causal speculation, hearsay, circumlocution	○ / ○	○ / ○	らむ / (らん)	らむ / (らん)	らめ / ○	○ / ○	*yodan*	SS (RT of RH)
けむ (9.3)	Speculative past, causal conjecture, past hearsay	けま / ○	○ / ○	けむ / (けん)	けむ / (けん)	けめ / ○	○ / ○		RY

Aux. verb	Functions	MZ	RY	SS	RT	IZ	MR	Conj.	Follows
めり (9.8)	Visual supposition, circumlocution	◯	めり	めり	める	めれ	◯	*rahen*	SS (RT of RH)
べし (9.7)	Conjecture with confidence, strong intention, appropriateness, advice, command, potential	◯ べから	べく べかり	べし ◯	べき べかる	べけれ ◯	◯ ◯	*ku* adj.	SS (RT of RH)
らし (9.5)	Evidential supposition	◯	◯	らし	らし	らし	◯	Special	
まし (9.6)	Counterfactual speculation, desire for hypothetical state, hesitation	(ませ) ましか	◯ ◯	◯ まし	◯ まし	◯ ましか	◯ ◯	Special	MZ
なり (9.9)	Hearsay, aural supposition, direct hearing	◯	なり	なり	なる	なれ	◯	*rahen*	SS (RT of RH)
ず (6.1)	Negation	(な) ◯ ざら	(に) ず ざり	◯ ず ◯	ぬ ◯ ざる	ね ◯ ざれ	◯ ◯ ざれ	Special	MZ
じ (10.1.1)	Negative speculation, negative intention	◯	◯	じ	じ	じ	◯	Special	MZ
まじ (10.1.2)	Negative speculation, negative intention, inappropriateness, negative potential, prohibition	◯ まじから	まじく まじかり	まじ ◯	まじき まじかる	まじけれ ◯	◯ ◯	*shiku* adj.	SS (RT of RH)
まほし (10.2.2)	First-person desire, third-person desire, situational desire	◯ まほしから	まほしく まほしかり	まほし ◯	まほしき まほしかる	まほしけれ ◯	◯ ◯	*shiku* adj.	MZ
たし (10.2.1)		◯ たから	たく たかり	たし ◯	たき たかる	たけれ ◯	◯ ◯	*ku* adj.	RY
なり (8.1)	Copula, location, naming	なら ◯	なり に	なり ◯	なる ◯	なれ ◯	なれ ◯	*nari* adj. verb	RT, nominals
たり (8.2)	Copula	たら ◯	たり と	たり ◯	たる ◯	たれ ◯	たれ ◯	*tari* adj. verb	Nominals
ごとし (10.3)	Comparison, example	◯	ごとく	ごとし	ごとき	◯	◯	*ku* adj.	RT, nominals, particles *no* and *ga*
ゆ (20.1.1)	Passive, potential, spontaneous	え	え	ゆ	ゆる	ゆれ	◯	*shimonidan*	MZ of YD, NH, RH
らゆ (20.1.1)		らえ	◯	◯	(らゆる)	◯	◯		MZ of SN
す (20.1.2)	Light honorific	さ	し	す	す	せ	せ	*yodan*	MZ of YD and SH
ふ (20.1.3)	Repeated action	は	ひ	ふ	ふ	へ	◯	*yodan*	MZ of YD

Table 5

AUXILIARY VERB TYPES AND FUNCTIONS

General categories	Auxiliary verbs	Primary functions	Conjugation	Inflection followed
Spontaneous, potential, passive, honorific (自発, 可能, 受身, 尊敬)	る	Spontaneous, potential, passive, honorific	*shimo-nidan*	MZ of YD, NH, RH verbs
	らる			MZ of verbs other than the above
Causative, honorific (使役, 尊敬)	す	Causative, honorific		MZ of YD, NH, RH verbs
	さす			MZ of verbs other than the above
	しむ			MZ
Perfective (完了)	つ	Perfective, certainty, parallel	*shimo-nidan*	RY
	ぬ		*nahen*	
	たり	Resultative, continuative, perfective	*rahen*	
	り	Resultative, continuative, perfective		IZ of *yodan* (MZ of *sahen*)
Recollective (回想)	き	Personal past	Special	RY (special after *kahen* and *sahen*)
	けり	Past hearsay, exclamatory, recognition, direct past	*rahen*	RY
	む	Speculation, intention, appropriateness, urging, circumlocution, hypothetical	*yodan*	MZ
	むず	Intention, speculation	*sahen*	
Speculative (推量)	らむ	Present speculation, causal speculation, hearsay, circumlocution	*yodan*	SS (RT of *rahen*)
	けむ	Speculation about past, causal conjecture, past hearsay		RY
	めり	Visual supposition, circumlocution	*rahen*	SS (RT of *rahen*)
	べし	Conjecture with confidence, strong intention, appropriateness, advice, command, potential	*ku* adj.	SS (RT of *rahen*)
	らし	Evidential supposition	Special	
	まし	Counterfactual speculation, desire for hypothetical state, hesitation	Special	MZ

General categories	Auxiliary verbs	Primary functions	Conjugation	Inflection followed
Hearsay (伝聞) でんぶん	なり	Hearsay, aural supposition, direct hearing	*rahen*	SS (RT of *rahen*)
Negative (打消) うちけし	ず	Negation	Special	MZ
Negative speculative (打消推量) うちけしすいりょう	じ	Negative speculation, negative intention	Special	MZ
	まじ	Negative speculation, negative intention, inappropriateness, negative potential, prohibition	*shiku* adj.	SS (RT of *rahen*)
Desiderative (希望) きぼう	まほし	First-person desire, third-person desire, situational desire	*shiku* adj.	MZ
	たし		*ku* adj.	RY
Copular (断定) だんてい	なり	Copula, location, naming	*nari* adj. verb	RT, nominals
	たり	Copula	*tari* adj. verb	Nominals
Comparative (比況) ひきょう	ごとし	Comparison, example	*ku* adj.	RT, nominals, particles *no* and *ga*

Table 6

AUXILIARY VERB CONNECTIONS

Follows these inflected forms					Follows noninflected forms
Mizenkei	*Ren'yōkei*	*Shūshikei**	*Rentaikei*	*Izenkei/ meireikei*	
る らる す さす しむ む むず まし ず じ まほし	つ ぬ たり (resultative) き けり けむ たし	らむ めり べし らし まじ なり (hearsay)	なり (copular) ごとし	り	なり (copular) たり (copular) ごとし

*After *rahen*, all of these follow the *rentaikei*.

Table 7

PARTICLES

		Case particles (格助詞<ruby>かくじょし</ruby>)			
	Chap. sec.	Function	Follows	Modern Japanese	English
が	12.1	1. Subject marker		1. が	1. —
		2. Attributive marker		2. の	2. of
		3. Implied nominal		3. のもの	3. that of
の	12.2	1. Subject marker	Nominals, RT	1. が	1. —
		2. Attributive marker		2. の	2. at, of
		3. Implied nominal		3. のもの	3. that of
を	12.3	1. Object of action		1. を	1. —
		2. Point of transit		2. を	2. through
		3. Point of origin		3. から	3. from
		4. Marks object of causative action		4. を	4. to have . . . do
		5. Assumption		5. を . . . として	5. assuming that
		6. Cause		6. が . . . なので	6. because, since
に	12.4	1. Place of action	Nominals, RT	1. に	1. at, on, in
		2. Time of action		2. に, ときに	2. at, in
		3. Destination or direction of action		3. に, の方<ruby>ほう</ruby>に	3. at, to
		4. Target of action		4. に	4. on, at, to
		5. Cause, origin, or purpose of action		5. のために, によって	5. because of, in order to
		6. Result of a change		6. になる	6. turn into, become
		7. Means of action		7. で, によって	7. with, by means of
		8. Object of causative or passive		8. に	8. by
		9. Standard of comparison		9. より, と比<ruby>くら</ruby>べて	9. more than, compared with
		10. Position, qualification		10. として	10. as
		11. Addition		11. に, のうえに	11. on the top of
へ	12.5	Direction or destination	Nominals	へ, の方<ruby>ほう</ruby>に	to

Case particles (格助詞)

	Chap. sec.	Function	Follows	Modern Japanese	English
と	12.6	1. Action taken with another	Nominals, RT, citation	1. とともに	1. together with
		2. Parallel items		2. と	2. and
		3. Content citation		3. と言って	3. ".."
		4. Result of change		4. に	4. to become
		5. Metaphor		5. のように	5. like
		6. Standard of comparison		6. と比べて	6. compared with
		7. Objective of action		7. しようとして	7. with the aim of
		8. To regard X as Y		8. として	8. as
		9. Without exception		9. すべて	9. all
より	12.7	1. Point of origin		1. から	1. from
		2. Standard of comparison		2. より	2. superior to
		3. Means, method		3. で, によって	3. by
		4. Point of transit		4. を通って	4. through
		5. Two actions in rapid sequence		5. とすぐに	5. as soon as
		6. Restriction, limitation		6. よりほかに	6. except for
から	12.8	1. Point of origin		1. から	1. from
		2. Means, method	Nominals, RT	2. で, によって	2. by, with
		3. Passage		3. を通して	3. via, through
		4. Cause or origin of action		4. によって	4. because
		5. Rapid sequence		5. につれて	5. as soon as
にて	12.10	1. Indicates place, time, age		1. で	1. at
		2. Means, materials		2. で	2. with
		3. Cause, reason		3. によって	3. because
		4. Condition, qualification, status, role		4. として	4. as
して	12.9	1. Means, method	Nominals	1. で, を用いて	1. with, by
		2. Acting together		2. といっしょに	2. together with
		3. Object of causative action		3. に命じて	3. to make someone do something

Conjunctive particles (接続助詞)
_{せつぞくじょし}

	Chap. sec.	Function	Follows	Modern Japanese	English
ば	13.1	Logical connection based on a hypothetical situation	MZ	ならば, なら	if . . . then . . .
		Logical connection based on an existing situation	IZ		
		1. Causal		1. ので	1. since
		2. Temporal or random		2. と, ところ	2. when, happen to
		3. General rule		3. 時はいつも	3. it is a general rule that
		4. Parallel contrast		4. すると, 一方では	4. as this . . . that
と, とも	13.2	1. Concessive connection based on a hypothetical situation	SS (RY of adj.)	1. たとえ . . . しても	1. for example, even if
		2. Emphatic function		2. たとえそうであっても	2. though it may be the case that . . .
ど, ども	13.3	1. Concessive connection	IZ	けれども	though, but
に	13.4	1. Causal connection	RT	1. ので, ために	1. since, because
を	13.4	2. Concessive connection		2. のに, けれど	2. despite, though
		3. Simple connection		3. が, と	3. and, when, upon
		4. Additional		4. のに加えて	4. in addition, on top of that
が	13.5	1. Concessive connection	RT	1. が, のに, けれども	1. but, though
		2. Temporal, sequential connection		2. たところ, が	2. and, when
て	13.6	1. Temporal/sequential	RY	1. して, それから	1. and then
して	13.6	2. Simultaneous		2. で, て	2. at the same time
		3. Causal		3. ので, ために	3. therefore
		4. Existing condition		4. の状況で	4. being
		5. Concessive		5. のに	5. but, though, despite
で	13.7	Negative connection	MZ	ないで, なくて	not . . .
つつ	13.8	1. Repetitive or continuous action	RY	1. 何度も	1. repeatedly, continuously
		2. Simultaneous, parallel action		2. ながら	2. while

Conjunctive particles (接続助詞<ruby>せつぞくじょし</ruby>)

	Chap. sec.	Function	Follows	Modern Japanese	English
ながら	13.9	1. Simultaneous, parallel action	Word stem or RY	1. するとともに	1. while at the same time
		2. Concessive connection		2. が, ものの	2. though
		3. In the same state		3. ままで	3. as before
		4. All inclusive		4. 全部<ruby>ぜんぶ</ruby>	4. all
ものを, ものから, ものの, ものゆゑ	13.10	Concessive connection based on an existing situation	RT	のに, けれども	though, but

Bound particles (係助詞<ruby>かかりじょし</ruby>)

	Chap. sec.	Function	Follows	Modern Japanese	English
は	14.1	1. Topic marker		1. というものは	1. as for
		2. Distinction and emphasis		2. については特に<ruby>とく</ruby>	2. in particular
		3. Parallel		3. は	3. as for this . . . as for that . . .
も	14.2	1. Parallel listing		1. . . . も . . . も	1. and
		2. Incremental		2. も	2. also, too
		3. Emphatic, emotive		3. もまあ	3. My! What!
		4. Outer limit		4. も, さえも	4. even
		5. Anxiety (followed by *zo* or *koso*)	Various words	5. したら困る<ruby>こま</ruby>	5. it would be terrible if . . .
ぞ	14.3	1. Emphatic		1. だぞ, なのだ	1. definitely, for sure
		2. Anxiety (preceded by *mo*)		2. . . . しては困る<ruby>こま</ruby>	2. there is a danger that
		3. Abbreviated ending		3. —	3. —
なむ なん	14.4	1. Emphatic		1. だぞ	1. indeed
		2. Abbreviated ending		2. —	2. —
や やは	14.5	1. Doubt, question		1. か, だろうか	1. "?"
		2. Rhetorical question		2. か . . . いや . . . ではない	2. Does it? (No, it does not.)

Bound particles (係 助詞)

<ruby>係 助詞<rt>かかり じょし</rt></ruby>

	Chap. sec.	Function	Follows	Modern Japanese	English
か かは	14.6	1. Doubt, question 2. Rhetorical question	Various words	1. か, だろうか 2. か…いや… ではない	1. "?" 2. Does it? (No, it does not.)
こそ	14.7	1. Strong emphasis 2. Concessive 3. Hailing 4. Abbreviated ending 5. Anxiety (preceded by *mo*)		1. その物・その人 2. は…だけれど 3. よ 4. — 5. すると困る	1. precisely 2. but, though 3. — 4. — 5. if … were to … it would be bad

Adverbial particles (副助詞)

<ruby>副助詞<rt>ふくじょし</rt></ruby>

	Chap. sec.	Function	Follows	Modern Japanese	English
し しも	15.8	1. Emphasis 2. Limited situation 3. Emphatic negation		1. れが 2. に限って 3. 決して…ない	1. precisely 2. only then 3. absolutely (not)
すら	15.1	1. Minimal example 2. Minimal desire		1. さえ, でさえ 2. せめて, だけでも	1. even X, how much more Y 2. at least, even
だに	15.2	1. Minimal need, lower limit 2. Minimal example	Various words	1. せめて…だけでも 2. さえ, でさえ	1. at the very least 2. even X, not to mention Y
さへ	15.3	1. Addition 2. Minimal example		1. そのうえ 2. でさえも	1. in addition 2. even X, not to mention Y
のみ	15.4	1. Limitation 2. Emphasis 3. Emphasizes the intensity and continuous nature of a state or action		1. だけ, ばかり 2. とくに 3. ひたすら	1. only 2. particularly 3. nothing but

Adverbial particles (副助詞)

	Chap. sec.	Function	Follows	Modern Japanese	English
ばかり	15.5	1. Approximation		1. あたり, ごろ, くらい	1. about, around
		2. Extent/degree of an action or situation		2. ほど, ぐらい	2. to the extent that
		3. Restriction		3. だけ	3. only
		4. Minimal extent		4. にすぎない	4. no more than
		5. Intense repetition	Various	5. 専ら	5. nothing but
まで	15.7	1. Scope, limit	words	1. まで, かぎり	1. until, to, up to
		2. Unexpected degree or state		2. ほどに, ぐらいまで	2. so much so that, to the point that
など	15.6	1. Example from a group of similar items		1. など, なんか	1. and such
		2. Circumlocution		2. など	2. and such
		3. Citation		3. などと	3. to say such things as

Final particles (終助詞)

	Chap. sec.	Function	Follows	Modern Japanese	English
か	16.1.1	Exclamation	Nominals, RT	よ, だなあ	!!
かな	16.1.1				
な	16.1.2	1. Exclamation	Nominals, end of sentence	1. よ, なあ, ことだなあ	1. !!
		2. Seeking assurance, confirmation		2. な, だな, だね	2. Is it true that? Am I right?
な	16.1.3	Negative imperative	SS (RT of RH)	...な	Don't...!
そ	16.1.4	Negative imperative	RY (MZ of NH and SH)	...な, ...しないでくれ	Please don't...!
かし	16.1.5	1. Emphasis	End of sentence	1. ね, よ, ことだ	1. You know that.
		2. Self-confirmation		2....なのだな	2. My...

Final particles (終助詞<ruby>しゅうじょし</ruby>)

	Chap. sec.	Function	Follows	Modern Japanese	English
なむ (なん)	16.1.6	Request or desire with regard to other people or things	MZ	してほしい	I wish that . . . would
ばや	16.1.7	1. First-person desire 2. Desire to see a situation realized 3. Intention	MZ	1. . . . たいものだ 2. . . . があればよい がなあ 3. . . . よう	1. I want to . . . 2. I wish that . . . would 3. I intend to
がな もがな	16.1.8	Expresses hope or desire with regard to a situation that is unlikely to occur	Nominals, RY, etc.	. . . がほしいなあ, . . . あったらなあ	If only . . .
てしが てしがな にしが にしがな	16.1.9 ——— 16.1.10	First-person desire or wish	RY	. . . したいものだ	I want

Interjectory particles (間投助詞<ruby>かんとうじょし</ruby>)

	Chap. sec.	Function	Follows	Modern Japanese	English
や	16.2.1	1. Exclamation 2. Address, summons 3. Cutting word 4. Rhythm	Middle or end of sentence	1. だなあ 2. よ 3. ことよ 4. —	1. ! 2. You there. 3. — 4. —
よ	16.2.2	1. Address, summons 2. Exclamation 3. Reinforcement of command		1. よ 2. な, よ 3. よ	1. You there. 2. ! 3. !
を	16.2.3	1. Exclamation 2. Emphasis		1. ね, よ 2. —	1. ! 2. —

Nara-Period case particles (格助詞<ruby>かくじょし</ruby>)

	Chap. sec.	Function	Follows	Modern Japanese	English
ゆ ゆり よ	20.2.1	1. Starting point 2. Point of transit 3. Means, method	Nominals, RT	1. から 2. を通<ruby>とお</ruby>って 3. で	1. from 2. through 3. by, with
つ	20.2.2	Attributive indicating place, time, possession, or attribution	Nominals	の	of, from

Nara-Period auxiliary verbs

	Chap. sec.	Function	MZ	RY	SS	RT	IZ	MR	Conj.	Follows
ゆ	20.1.1	Passive, potential, spontaneous	え	え	ゆ	ゆる	ゆれ	○	*shimo-nidan*	MZ of YD, NH, RH
らゆ	20.1.1		らえ	○	○	(らゆる)	○	○		MZ of SN
す	20.1.2	Light honorific	さ	し	す	す	せ	せ	*yodan*	MZ of YD and SH
ふ	20.1.3	Repeated action	は	ひ	ふ	ふ	へ	○	*yodan*	MZ of YD

Nara-Period final particles (終助詞)

	Chap. sec.	Function	Follows	Modern Japanese	English
かも	20.3.1	1. Exclamation 2. Question or exclamatory rhetorical question	Nominals, RT	1. だなあ 2. (の) かなあ	1. ! 2. I wonder if . . .
な	20.3.2	1. First-person intention or desire 2. Invitation to do something together 3. Request	MZ	1. . . . たいなあ 2. . . . しようよ 3. . . . してほしい	1. I want to . . . 2. Let us . . . 3. Please . . .
なも	20.3.3	Request	MZ	. . . てほしい	I wish that . . .
ね	20.3.4	Request	MZ	. . . てほしい	I wish that . . .
もが もがも	20.3.5	First-person desire for something unlikely to happen	Nominals, RY, particles	. . . があったらなあ	If only . . .
も	20.3.6	Exclamation	End of sentence	よ	!
こそ	20.3.7	Desire or wish with regard to others	RY	. . . てほしい	I wish that . . .
しか てしか	20.3.8, 20.3.9	Wish that is difficult to obtain	RY	. . . たらいいのに	If only . . .
そ	20.3.10	Declarative	Nominals RT	だよ	it is . . .

Nara-Period bound particles (係助詞<ruby>かかりじょし</ruby>)

Chap. sec.	Function	Modern Japanese	English
そ 20.4.1	Emphatic	だぞ, なのだ	definitely

Table 8

MAIN FUNCTIONS OF INFLECTED FORMS

mizenkei (未然形)	Negation when followed by auxiliary verb *zu* 皆人見知らず. *No one* recognized it. (*Ise*, sec. 9, NKBT 9:117)
	Intention, conjecture, or desire when followed by auxiliary verb *mu* (intention), *ji* (negative intention), *mashi* (conjecture), or *mahoshi* (desire) 乙女のすがたしばしとどめん. *I want to* keep the image of the young women for a while. (*KKS*, Misc. 1, no. 872, NKBT 8:277)
	Hypothetical situation when followed by conjunctive particle *ba* 心あらば . . . *If you have* a heart . . . (*Shūishū*, Autumn, Misc., no. 1128, SNKT 7:323)
	Desire or request when followed by final particles *baya* and *namu* いかで見ばやと思ひつつ. I was thinking how much *I would like* to see the (tales). (*Sarashina*, NKBT 20:479)
	Potential, passive, spontaneous, honorific, and causative functions when followed by auxiliary verbs *ru, raru, su, sasu,* and *shimu. Ru* and *raru* are potential, passive, spontaneous, and honorific, while *su, sasu,* and *shimu* are causative and honorific
ren'yōkei (連用形)	Modifies what follows, with verb or adjective assuming adverbial function 滝の糸は絶えて久しくなりぬれど . . . Though it has been *a long time* since the thread of the waterfall disappeared . . . (*Shūishū*, Misc. 1, no. 449, SNKBT 7:127)
	Indicates simultaneous or sequential action 炭山を越え, 笠取を過ぎて . . . We *crossed* Sumiyama and *passed* Kasatori . . . (*Hōjōki*, NKBT 30:39)

Perfective indicating completed action when followed by auxiliary verbs *ki,* *keri, tsu, nu, tari,* and *kemu.* (*Tsu* and *nu* can also express certainty.)

Desiderative when followed by auxiliary verb *tashi,* final particles *teshigana* and *nishigana,* or final particle *mogana* (after adjective)

世の中に さらぬ別れの なくもがな. *I wish* the parting that we cannot avoid in this world was not to be. (*Ise,* sec. 84, NKBT 9:162)

Consecutive or simultaneous action when followed by conjunctive particles *te, tsutsu,* and *nagara*

Prohibitive when followed by final particle *so* (as in *na . . . so*)

今日, 波な立ちそ. Today, *stop* the waves. (*Tosa,* NKBT 20:50–51)

Hypothetical concessive when adjective is followed by conjunctive particle *tomo*

吉野川水のこころははやくとも . . . *Even if* the heart of the water of the Yoshino River is swift . . . (*KKS,* Love 3, no. 651, NKBT 8:231)

Hypothetical when *ren'yōkei* of adjective or negative auxiliary verb *zu* is followed by bound particle *wa*

こひしくはとぶらひきませ. *If you should be* lovesick, please come and visit. (*KKS,* Misc. 2, no. 982, NKBT 8:301)

Nominalizing function when *ren'yōkei* of verb is followed by case particle *ni*

暇 あらば拾ひに行かむ. If I have time, I will go *to pick it up.* (*MYS,* vol. 7, no. 1147, NKBT 5:215)

shūshikei (終止形)	End of sentence, indicating current action. Dictionary form いささかに雨降る. The rain *falls* little by little. (*Tosa,* NKBT 20:38)

Speculative when followed by auxiliary verbs *ramu, rashi, beshi, maji, meri,* and *nari* (hearsay/supposition)

男 もすなる日記 . . . The diaries (*niki*) that *I hear* men keep . . . (*Tosa,* NKBT 20:27)

Doubt/rhetorical question when followed by bound particle *ya*

有りやなしや. Is (she) alive or dead? (*KKS,* Travel, no. 411, NKBT 8:186)

Prohibition when followed by final particle *na*

あやまちすな! *Do not* make a mistake! (*Tsurezure,* sec. 109, NKBT 30:178)

Hypothetical concessive when followed by conjunctive particle *tomo*, "even if"

ちりぬとも香をだに残せ. *Even if* the (blossoms) end up scattering, at least leave (*nokose*) the scent (*ka*). (*KKS*, Spring 1, no. 48, NKBT 8:113)

---

rentaikei
(連体形)

Direct modifier when followed by nominal

ひとり寝る夜. A night (*yo*) when one *sleeps* (*nuru*) alone (*hitori*). (*Shūishū*, Love 4, no. 912, SNKBT 7:912)

Nominalizer when followed by case particle

さくらの花のちるをよめる. Composed on the *scattering* (*chiru*) of the blossoms (*hana*) of the cherry tree. (*KKS*, Spring 2, no. 84, NKBT 8:118)

Sentence ending when preceded by bound particles *zo*, *namu*, *ya*, or *ka*

秋は色々の花にぞありける. As for autumn (*aki*), it has flowers (*hana*) of different colors! (*KKS*, Autumn 1, no. 245, NKBT 8:149)

Exclamatory when followed by final particle *ka* or *kana*

うつせみの世にもにたるか. How it resembles (*ni-taru*) the world (*yo*) of the empty cicada (*utsusemi*)! (*KKS*, Spring 2, no. 73, NKBT 8:117)

Speculation when *rentaikei* of *rahen* verb is followed by speculative auxiliary verbs *ramu*, *rashi*, *beshi*, *maji*, *meri*, or *nari* (hearsay)

Sentence ending when preceded by question word

などわが宿に一声もせぬ. Why (*nado*) has the (cuckoo) *not* sung once (*hito-koe-se-nu*) at my lodge (*yado*)? (*SKKS*, Summer, no. 189, NKBT 28:71)

---

izenkei
(已然形)

Logical connection when followed by conjunctive particle *ba*, "since," "when"

この子を見れば, 苦しき事もやみぬ. *When* he looked at this child, (his) suffering disappeared. (*Taketori*, NKBT 9:30)

Resultative/continuative/perfective when followed by auxiliary verb *ri*

若草のつまもこもれり我もこもれり. Both my wife (*tsuma*) of the young grass (*wakakusa*) and I (*ware*) *are* hid*ing* here (*komore-ri*). (*KKS*, Spring 1, no. 17, NKBT 8:108)

Concessive when followed by conjunctive particle *do* or *domo*

男も女も恥ぢ交はしてありけれ<u>ど</u> . . . *Though* the man and the woman

were embarrassed with each other . . . (*Ise*, sec. 23, NKBT 9:126)

Emphatic, at end of sentence and preceded by bound particle *koso*

折節の移りかはる<u>こそ</u>, ものごとに哀なれ. It is *precisely* the changing of

the seasons that makes everything so moving. (*Tsurezure*, sec. 19, NKBT

30:104)

Concessive, in middle of sentence preceded by *koso*

人<u>こそ</u>見え<u>ね</u>秋は来にけり. *Though* no one appeared, autumn has come.

(*Shūishū*, Autumn, no. 140, SNKBT 7:42)

| *meireikei* (命令形) | Imperative
汝, よく聞け. Hey you (*nanji*), *listen* closely! (*Konjaku*, vol. 2, NKBT 22:165) |